Jersey Evening Post

Images of Jersey

Images of Jersey

Jersey Evening Post

The
Breedon Books
Publishing Company
Derby

First published in Great Britain by
The Breedon Books Publishing Company Limited
44 Friar Gate, Derby, DE1 1DA
1994

ISBN 1 873626 80 0

Printed and bound by Hillman Printers, Frome, Somerset.
Covers printed by BDC Printing Services Limited of Derby

Contents

Foreword

THE history of the 20th century will differ from that of any previous period in that it can be recorded with photographic images. The photographic process was invented in the middle of the 1800s but it was to be the turn of the century before its use became sufficiently widespread to become part of everyday life.

It is mainly through newspapers that photographs have provided in this century a unique record of public life and the Jersey Evening Post's own archives provide by far the most detailed history available of the life of a rapidly changing island community.

A community which has seen its principal source of revenue change first from agriculture to tourism and then to international finance has seen equally dramatic changes in appearance and these have been recorded down the years by the cameras of Jersey Evening Post photographers.

For the first time a representative selection of the tens of thousands of pictures they have produced have been gathered together in this volume which, as well as representing a small part of the newspaper's own contribution to the history of 20th century Jersey, provides a fascinating insight for islanders and visitors of how the Jersey they know and love has changed and developed over the years.

Mike Bisson
Editor
Jersey Evening Post
July 1994

Introduction

JERSEY is an island rich in images, history, prehistory, tradition and lore. It is also unique in so many ways, with its own language, its right to be part of the British Isles yet separate from the United Kingdom, its distinctly Anglo-French flavour and its special climate, always that much warmer because of its southerly position and the moderating influence of the Gulf Stream.

Yet this very small piece of sea-locked land, a mere nine miles by five with a population no greater than the average English provincial town, is wholly responsible for its own government, in the shape of the States of Jersey, has a highly successful finance industry with a worldwide reputation, a unique horticultural and agricultural industry, and is a holiday island with a very special atmosphere.

With a population of just over 80,000, the Island runs its own international airport, harbour, customs and police force. The last of these is yet another of Jersey's special attributes, being divided into the States Police Force, who are paid and wear uniform, and the Honorary Police, a civilian body, each member of which is elected by the people. Interestingly, this system may now be experimented with in parts of the UK.

The Island is governed by unpaid, democratically elected politicians who are responsible for formulating and passing laws. They are nevertheless answerable in the final instance to the Crown, regarded by Islanders as their Duke of Normandy.

Jersey has an established reputation as a holiday centre for UK and Continental visitors. In addition, there are firm connections with many parts of the world through emigration, in particular in Canada, Australia and, of course, that part of the United States named after the Island, New Jersey.

The name Jersey, meanwhile, is known throughout the world thanks to the Island's most famous denizen, the beautiful Jersey cow, whose butterfat yield is unequalled by any other breed.

And many a fisherman has reason to be grateful for the warmth of his oiled wool jersey, a garment so successful that it has given its name to an entire category of clothing.

Jersey Royal new potatoes are also famous – and deservedly, because they have a taste which no other potato can match.

To sum up the nature of Jersey in a single collection of photographs would be impossible but this selection, taken from the archives of the Jersey Evening Post, gives at least a hint of the richness of Island life.

All the pictures were either taken by the newspaper's staff photographers or have, over the years, been donated to the newspaper's archives by its readers.

It is hoped that they will give an accurate impression of a small yet by no means insignificant part of the world which is beautiful, happy and which always offers a warm welcome to visitors – wherever they may come from.

Gordon Young,
March 1994

Royalty

King George V is presented with a Jersey cow at Springfield in 1921.

In 1957, King George V's granddaughter, Queen Elizabeth II, is presented with a Jersey.

King George V and Queen Mary meet Islanders at a Government House garden party in 1921.

Halberdiers form an arch of honour for their majesties at Mont Orgueil Castle.

Queen Mary signs the visitors' book on a table laid out beneath the castle trees at Mont Orgueil.

The seat of the 'royal' Wolseley 14/40 got rather too hot for Queen Mary on an Island tour and she threw the cushions overboard en route.

The young cadets of the Officer Training Corps at Victoria College are inspected by a royal visitor.

At St Helier Harbour His Majesty inspects World War One veterans.

The Princess Royal inspects the Girl Guides of Jersey during the 1921 visit.

Above: King George VI and Queen Elizabeth arrive at Jersey Airport on 7 June 1945, less than a month after the building was occupied by German forces.

Left: Princess Margaret is pictured with the Lt-Governor, Admiral Sir Gresham Nicholson, and the Bailiff of Jersey, Sir Alexander Coutanche, on her visit in 1956.

Princess Anne makes the acquaintance of a very small monkey held in the capable hands of author and Jersey Zoo director Gerald Durrell.

Princess Elizabeth and her husband Prince Philip pose with the official party at Government House in 1949.

The children enjoy the novelty of a street party to celebrate the Coronation of Queen Elizabeth II on 2 June 1953.

The Queen and the Duke of Edinburgh pose for the photographers outside the States Building in 1957.

Earl Mountbatten of Burma inspects the parade of the Victoria College Combined Cadet Force in 1962.

The Duke and Duchess of Gloucester with Victoria College headmaster Ronnie Postill.

Princess Margaret is pictured enjoying herself as she meets Eric Morecambe and his wife at a Variety Club charity weekend in Jersey.

The Queen Mother talks to Thomas J.King as a new Jersey lifeboat is named after him in 1957.

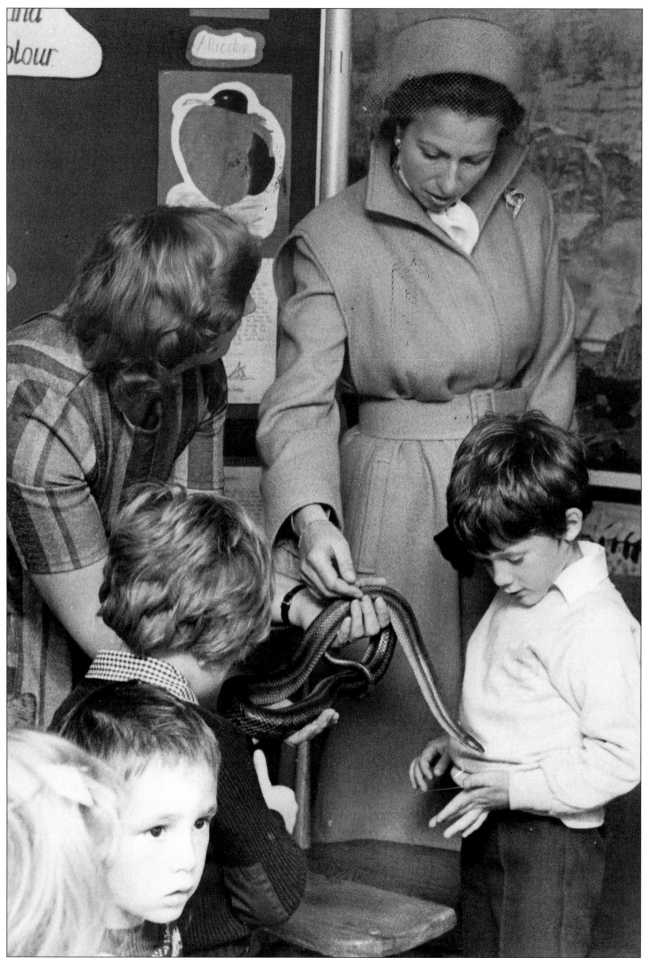

Princess Anne meets a king snake and some children at Les Landes School during her visit in 1984.

The delight of presenting a bouquet to the Queen Mother shows on the face of a little girl. Her male companion, meanwhile, is not quite so sure.

The Queen Mother is welcomed by the people of Jersey in the Royal Square as she stands on the balcony of the United Club in 1963.

The Queen Mother has the finer points of a traditional jersey explained to her by a Scout leader.

The Queen meets 100-year-old Miss Lilian Le Couteur in 1989.

Famous Visitors

Hollywood film star Deborah Kerr pays a visit to her Jersey-based sister, Lady Walker, in 1954.

Evening Post reporter Mike Rumfitt talks to author C.S.Forester, creator of the Horatio Hornblower series of sea adventures, on a visit in 1958.

Arthur 'I thank you!' Askey with daughter Anthea in Jersey in 1957.

Singer Frankie Vaughan was escort to Miss Jersey Battle of Flowers 1959, Maureen Whittingham.

Disc jockey Jimmy Savile escorted Miss Battle Carole Reeves in 1969.

James Robertson Justice of 'Doctor in the House' film fame was a guest of honour in 1958. Miss Battle was Peggy Poole.

In 1951 Hugh Gaitskell, Chancellor of the Exchequer and later Leader of the Labour Party, and his family came to stay in the Island.

Film star John Mills and his authoress wife Mary Hayley Bell spent a holiday in Jersey in 1949.

He came, he saw and he stayed. Alan Whicker on a visit in 1961. He liked Jersey so much that now he is an Island resident.

Gerald Durrell, in the fur-lined jacket, seen here with supporters at the Royal Court in 1971, not only settled in Jersey but also founded the world-famous Jersey Zoo.

The voice of cricket, John Arlott, seen here commentating at the 1958 Muratti (the annual Jersey-Guernsey soccer Derby) picked Alderney as his retirement home.

Left: Rock Hudson (right) was in Jersey to film Sea Devils, *a swashbuckling adventure story based on Victor Hugo's* Toilers of the Sea. *His co-star was Yvonne de Carlo.*

Below: Jack Hawkins, the English film star, was Mr Battle of Flowers in 1957 as escort to Miss Battle Jean Oeillet.

It was June Valerie Wilson who was the envy of all the women watching the Battle of Flowers parade when, as Miss Battle 1978, her escort was French heart-throb Sacha Distell.

The Battle of Flowers celebrity in 1956 was a woman, the gracious and regal film star Anna Neagle, who had portrayed Queen Victoria in Sixty Glorious Years.

Swedish film actress Mai Zetterling holds Jersey Zoo's baby gorilla, Npongo, with (on the left) Gerald Durrell and author Davis Hughes.

'Monty', Field Marshall Viscount Montgomery of Alamein, visits Jersey in 1949 and proves very popular with the crowds.

Monty signs the bass drum of the Junior Training Corps of Victoria College.

Agriculture

Threshing was by steam power at the end of the last century on this Jersey farm where the workers are pictured taking a break which was recorded on a glass plate for posterity.

Picking the famous Jersey Royal potato at the turn of the century. But was the formal dress purely for the benefit of the camera?

Traditional Jersey vans, loaded with barrels of new potatoes, queue to have their loads weighed, the drivers and horses showing the patience of those gentle farming days.

The Weighbridge was not just a functional machine – it was also the place for a good chat.

Queues of potato lorries waiting to use the Weighbridge could stretch for miles outside St Helier in a good year . . .

. . . and when your turn came it was a relief . . .

. . . but once the produce was weighed it still had to go aboard the boats which would take it to the UK.

Auctions of gift lots of potatoes donated by farmers for charity were a regular feature at the Weighbridge.

The traditional fertiliser for Jersey fields has always been the God-given seaweed or vraic which is gathered from the Island beaches with horse and cart – as here at Le Hocq at the turn of the century.

In the Fifties Jersey farmers were still gathering vraic in the traditional way.

The trip to the beach was an ideal opportunity for the horses to cool their hooves in the sea's edge.

'Forking spuds', the traditional way to dig new potatoes without bruising them. These two women wear traditional bonnets to protect them from the hot Jersey sun.

Planting Jersey Royal seed potatoes before machinery made the job easier.

Right: On the steep slopes of many Jersey fields – called côtils – machinery still had to give way to the traditional method.

Below: Ploughing the côtils needs a steady hand and a well disciplined horse – and it's never too soon to learn the job from Dad.

This young farmer, Ted Amy, ploughing his land at L'Etacq, favoured a single horse for planting potatoes.

Mr Perchard of La Hougue Farm preferred to use five horses to pull his plough.

Six fine beasts pulled the plough for Mr Perredes, of St Saviour, who had a helping hand to guide the huge team.

All work and no play makes Dobbin a dull horse, as this 1938 farm horse trotting race at Trinity shows.

Two Jersey beauties. Little Miss Perchard looks after award-winning Keepers Victorious Lady at a cattle show in 1953.

The traditional forge was still in action in 1958. Mr C.Villais, 70 years a blacksmith, is shown at work at his ancient trade.

Before and after the World War Two the seasonal farm workers were Bretons, who arrived by boat from France each year.

An Evening Post *reporter visits a Breton farmhouse to see what their home life was like.*

A traditional Jersey van piled with potatoes waiting on the docks for its load to be transferred to the ship.

By the time lorries were taking over from the traditional horse-drawn van, Jersey new potatoes were being shipped in barrels and sacks.

Battle of Flowers

The Battle of Flowers in 1906 consisted of a mixture of horse-drawn vehicles and early motor cars decorated with flowers.

By the Nineties the floats had become superb, sophisticated motorised works of floral art.

In 1953 there still was a genuine battle at the end of the parade, the spectators throwing flowers at each other, but hooliganism finally put a stop to that.

Petals from heaven, showers of paper pieces dropped from aircraft, was tried but it was messy and dangerous and the idea soon went out of favour.

Bigheads are a traditional part of the Battle and here they dwarf the Jersey Sea Cadet band.

Some famous people come to the Battle of Flowers – even, it seems, the world's leaders in 1961.

Above: This 1961 float shows a mystical chariot drawn by winged horses.

Right: The contestants for Miss Jersey Battle of Flowers in this picture did not need to spend a fortune on skirt material.

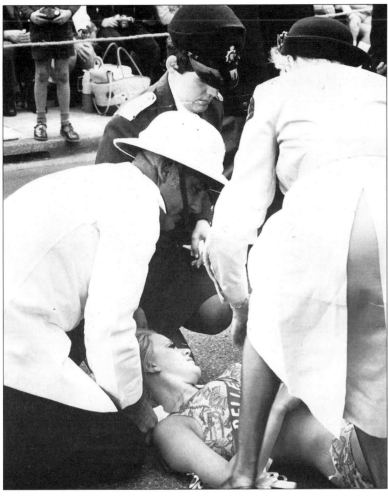

Left: Being a beauty queen in the cavalcade under the Jersey sun can be an exhausting experience but there is always the St John Ambulance Brigade or a handsome policeman to help.

Below: Miss Florence Bechelet is the longest-standing exhibitor in the Jersey Battle. Here she is in 1961 with one of her famous wild flower exhibits.

Floats in the Battle range from beautiful hand-drawn ones, such as 'The Joker's House', entered by individuals . . .

. . . to monsters such as the St Helier Parish float of 1963, which won the top prize – the Prix d'Honneur.

The runner-up, winner of the Prix d'Excellence, in 1965 was this float of the Black and White Minstrels, a popular TV show at the time.

Tiny huntsmen sit astride a wild flower float in the 1951 parade.

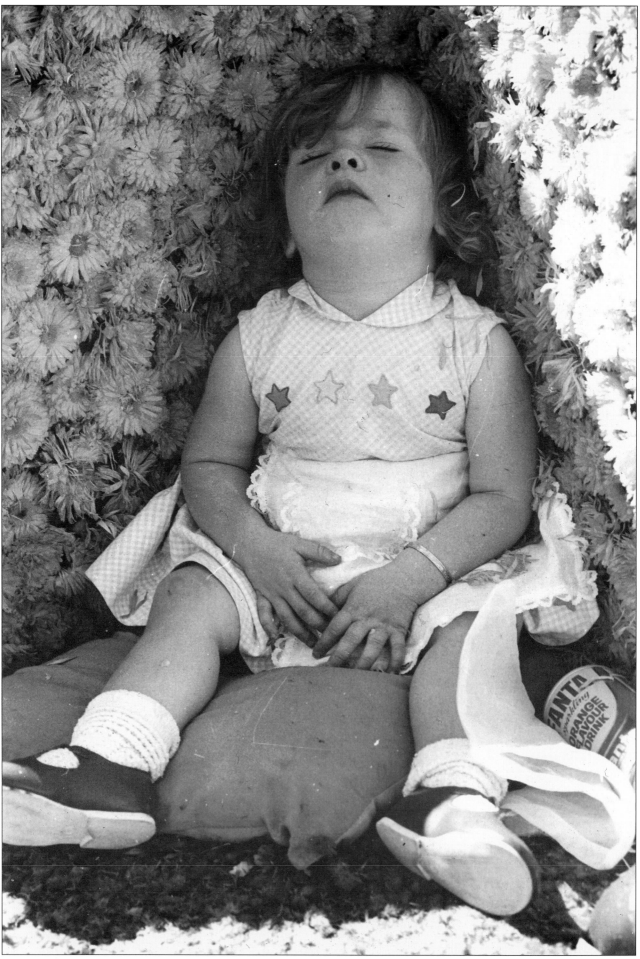

The Battle of Flowers parade proves a little too much for this tiny tot so she drops off on her flower-bedecked float.

The Sea

The master and officers of the SS Ibex, *a regular mailboat to Jersey, pose on board their vessel in 1897 . . . but all is not quite what it seems for, as can be seen below, the vessel was in trouble.*

Getting the Ibex *off the sands of Portelet beach where she went aground was no easy task – but she proved to be a great tourist attraction. She sank in 1900 off Guernsey after striking rocks.*

The paddle steamer Brittany *berths in St Helier Harbour in 1890.*

The ship that never went to sea was the naval training ship high on the hill above Gorey. The rigged masts presented a strange aspect.

The Isle of Guernsey, one of the great railway mailboats, sails past Elizabeth Castle into St Helier Harbour in 1959.

This novel method of sea transport from Gorey to France was tried but the hovercraft proved too noisy for the beach and the idea failed.

Vessels out of their time appeared off Elizabeth Castle in the early 1950s but it was all for the filming of the Sea Devils *with Rock Hudson.*

The film crew, perched precariously aboard an odd sailing vessel, film a sequence for the adventure story Sea Devils, *an adaptation of Victor Hugo's* Toilers of the Sea.

The St Helier lifeboat being launched in the early part of this century.

A fishing trawler runs aground and sinks just outside Rozel Harbour in March 1960.

The Jersey lifeboat William Henry Wilkinson *had to be manhandled to the sea on a huge-wheeled carriage in 1912.*

The Jersey lifeboat crew stand proudly before their new boat, Howard D, *a gift from T.B.Davis in memory of his son in 1937.*

Coxswain Thomas J.King (right) aboard the Howard D. *Later Tommy King would have a lifeboat named after him for his daring rescue of a yacht among the rocks off the Jersey coast.*

Above: The changing design of lifeboats can be seen in the Alexander Coutanche, pictured here in St Helier Harbour in 1990.

Left: Coxswain Thomas J.King wears the Gold Medal for conspicuous gallantry for rescuing the crew of the yacht Maurice Georges.

Clem Steele of St Brelade was still carrying on the traditional trade of making lobster pots in 1953.

The winners of the 1928 inter-insular rowing race, when Jersey beat Guernsey, bring their shell into St Helier Harbour.

Mr Le Masurier was hard at work in February 1952 fishing for ormers, the Channel Island shellfish delicacy. He is pictured practising the pastime in the traditional but very cold, wet and sometimes hazardous manner.

A mystery picture. It is uncertain who the eastern gent and his companions floating in their boat on the West Park Swimming Pool in the 1950s were, but they made an intriguing image.

The Military

The officers of the 1st Devonshire Regiment outside their barrack block at Grève de Lecq in 1911.

A barrack room scene at Grève de Lecq between 1903 and 1905 showing how the men slept, ate and lived in the same room.

'Sentence' about to be carried out after a mock court martial held by the 1st Devons around 1905.

The last garrison in Jersey, the 2nd Battalion the East Surreys, at the presentation of a silver cup at an unknown sporting event.

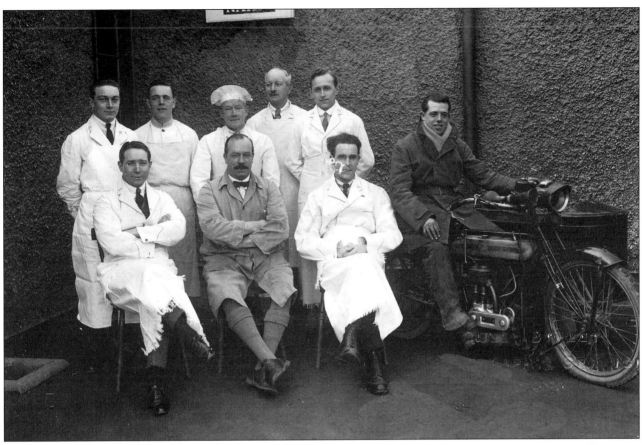

The British Army marches on its stomach and in 1924 the good old NAAFI and its staff were there to keep East Surreys happy.

'Goodbye Mary Ann, we must leave you' might have been what these lads were singing to their Jersey sweethearts as they set off for World War One.

The Royal Militia Island of Jersey march past St James' Church wearing full dress uniform. The year was 1914.

The YMCA were there to provide relaxing reading time for the troops on exercise at Le Quennevais in 1908.

Randall's Brewery Wet Canteen probably won plenty of custom if these two lads (attending after church parade) are anything to go by.

The smart young cadets of the Victoria College Officer Training Corps march home from a field day in March 1938.

Transport

When the baker called at the turn of the century he arrived wearing leather leggings in a splendid covered cart.

The Alberta carried passengers and mail to the Island. She is seen here in St Helier Harbour in 1900.

There is no tradesman's name on this rather ominous-looking vehicle standing outside Mr O'Brien's shop.

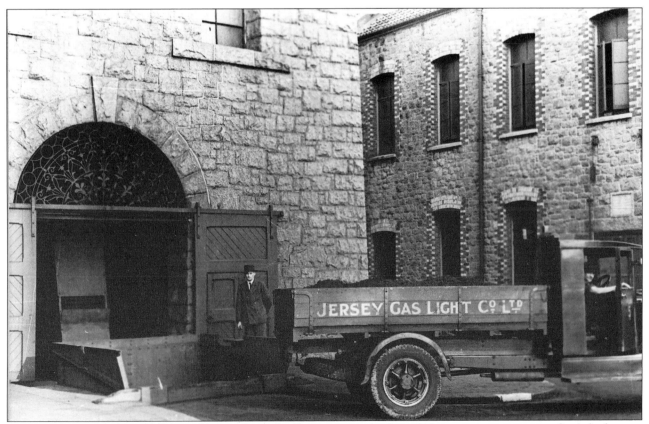

Coal was plentiful in 1940 for making gas but under German occupation it would become a very rare commodity indeed.

A far from common sight is a biplane in the middle of a town street. This one was pictured in Gloucester Street in the Thirties.

The Cloud of Iona, *pictured here in St Helier Harbour, was an amphibian passenger aircraft which overshot the Island on a stormy night in 1936.*

The wreckage of the Cloud of Iona *was discovered later on the Minquiers Reef. All ten passengers and crew were lost.*

Before 1937 all aircraft landed on the beach at West Park. Passengers and crew waited patiently on the sands to board while children played only a few feet from the aircraft.

The new Jersey Airport at St Peter was opened in 1937. De Havilland biplanes landed on grass instead of the sands of St Aubin's Bay.

Sometimes the landing aircraft came in a little too low over the approach road for comfort.

Pigs finally did have wings when the Airport began to handle cargo.

Dear old Father Christmas came in by plane and found an ecstatic crowd of children to welcome him in 1949.

This Flying Flea was photographed in 1936. Whether it ever flew we have been unable to find out.

An Evening Post *van headline in September 1939 tells of the advent of the World War Two – but Islanders had no idea then that they would become an outpost of the German Reich for five long years.*

The Occupation meant that compromises had to be made and this splendid Town Service bus was a joint effort between travel agents Bellinghams and the Jersey Motor Transport Co.

Lord St Helier, *Jersey's first steam fire engine, bought in 1905, was tragically sent to the scrapyard to be broken up in 1952.*

A train on the Jersey western railway can be seen arriving at West Park Station before steaming off to St Aubin.

St Aubin with, in the left foreground, the arched roof of the splendid railway terminus.

October 1936 and the magnificent arched roof of the St Aubin terminus has been destroyed by a disastrous fire which also damaged the Terminus Hotel.

The 1936 fire did so much damage at the St Aubin station that it was never reopened.

Being able to get a glimpse of the cockpit of a display team biplane at Jersey Airport is too much of a temptation for these two men.

Despite the existence of the Airport at St Peter, the beach was always a stand-by – as in the case of this Channel Island Airways de Havilland which landed in the fierce weather of February 1947.

Taking off on snow-covered sand was, perhaps surprisingly, no problem.

Jersey used to have two bus termini. The main one, serving the west and north was at the Weighbridge, where Queen Victoria on her pedestal kept a sharp eye on them. There were double and single-deckers in those days.

The bus terminus for the eastern part of the Island was in the old railway cutting at Snow Hill. The buses were unable to turn in the confined space so a wooden turntable was installed.

When the tunnel was cut through South Hill, east and west were linked and the two bus termini were amalgamated at the Weighbridge. The tunnel would not accommodate double-deckers so, sadly, Jersey bade farewell to them in February 1971, when they sailed away on the MV Nincop.

New turbines for the Jersey Electricity Company's power station proved a problem as the landing craft bringing them could not get into St Helier Harbour. The solution was to land them on the beach at La Haule, to the delight of sunbathing holidaymakers.

A dramatic new form of transport came to Jersey in 1964. A hydrofoil was faster and more like an aircraft than the usual passenger ships. Condor 1, *seen here showing her paces in company with a helicopter, was the first of a successful fleet of hydrofoils and multihull wavepiercers.*

Careful driving is always encouraged in Jersey but the odd episode occurs when someone tries to take a shortcut, as in this case at the Harbour.

This driver managed to wreck his lorry only days after the Island was liberated from German Occupation in 1945.

The Jersey International Road Races lasted from 1947 to 1949, when they ended with a tragic crash. They attracted top drivers. Pictured here is Prince Bira of Siam in the pits at West Park.

Jerseyman Frank Le Gallais drove for Lord Selsdon in the 1949 race.

L.Vieloresi can be seen here travelling at speed down Victoria Avenue in the 1948 race.

Racing cars line up on the grid at West Park for the start of the first race in 1947.

The Five Mile Road, running almost the length of the west coast, provided an ideal track for road sprints. Monsters such as this home-made car, with a lounge chair for a seat, thrilled the crowds.

Cars had improved by 1954, as can be seen from this image of a glorious Jaguar XK120.

Jersey's most famous race track is the International Hill Climb at Bouley Bay. In the 1950s people dot the hillside like daffodils as they watch a car take the top bend.

The sand races at St Ouen attracted cars of all types from the tiny home-made ones to great gleaming thoroughbreds. They all provided thrills and spills.

Bouley Bay provides a wonderful backdrop as a motorcyclist rounds the last bend of the hill climb.

The sheer grace of a 2,300cc supercharged Bugatti streaking up Bouley Bay Hill was one of the highlights of a hill climb in October 1946.

The Occupation

The first year of the World War Two saw people in Jersey doing much the same as their counterparts in the United Kingdom, forming air raid precaution (ARP) units.

The St Helier lads, with their ancient lorry and oilskin-covered hats, seem poorly equipped to counter Nazi invasion.

The Jersey Fire Service went through full training in gas masks to prepare for the possibility of a bombing raid.

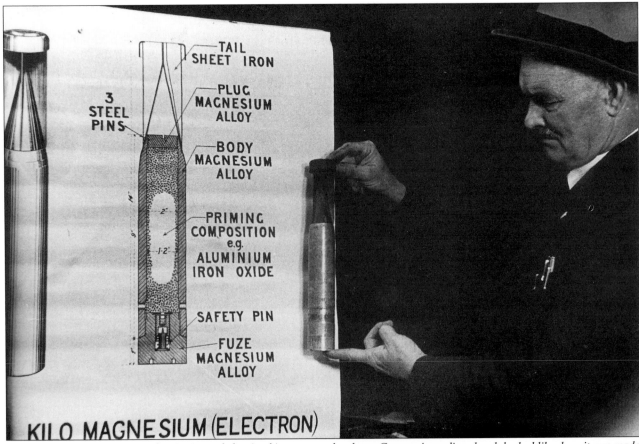

Jersey's ARP chief, Major Manley, is pictured showing his men exactly what a German incendiary bomb looked like, how it was made and how to deal with it.

Even the States of Jersey Police emerged in full air raid gear.

Air raid shelters were dug in the Parade Gardens.

As the Germans advanced towards the French coast it became obvious that they would invade Jersey. People who preferred to leave the Island for the United Kingdom thronged the Parade to register at the Town Hall.

When evacuation took place there were many sad sights. Here age and youth wait patiently to board a boat on the St Helier quayside.

Whole families waited patiently at the Harbour, their prams holding the few belongings they could manage to take.

The early part of 1940 saw many Jersey servicemen returning for leave in the Island. It was the last time that they would see their families for five long years.

*Yet another family is
separated for the
duration of the war.*

*On 1 July 1940 the German forces entered the demilitarised Channel Islands and for five years the Islanders suffered enemy
occupation — the only part of the British Isles to do so. Here a German band is pictured playing in the Royal Parade Gardens.*

Minefields and fortifications sprang up all over a previously free and happy holiday Island.

'Needs must' was the theme as fuel ran short and motor vehicles were converted from several horsepower to single horsepower. At least hay was plentiful at first.

*To avoid the
population
learning of
British victories
all wireless sets
were confiscated
by the Germans
so Islanders
made their own
crystal sets. Dick
Perchard shows
the one he used
to listen to the
BBC.*

*Fuel was in very short supply
so trees brought down in
storms provided an invaluable
source of heat for stoves and
fires.*

The Germans commandeered local vehicles and drivers. This magnificent Wolseley, originally brought to Jersey for a visit by the Prince of Wales, was used by the German Feld Kommandant. It is pictured here outside St Brelade's Church.

The dignity of dead British servicemen was maintained by the Germans, who buried them with full military honours. This is the funeral of two British airmen whose bodies were washed ashore — their coffins are draped with the Union Flag for the funeral at St Brelade's Church.

A.G.Harrison, the editor of the Evening Post, *had to deal with the problems of bringing out a newspaper under the supervision and censorship of the German occupying forces.*

By 1944 Islanders and occupiers were on the point of starvation. Only food parcels brought by the Swedish Red Cross ship Vega *saved the population.*

Every type of transportation was used to get the precious Red Cross parcels home.

It was on 9 May 1945, Liberation Day, that the first British troops landed to an ecstatic welcome from the Islanders.

On 8 May 1945 a huge crowd gathered in the Royal Square to hear Winston Churchill say on the BBC: ". . . and Our Dear Channel Islands are also to be freed today".

Some of the soldiers who liberated the Island were Jerseymen returning home.

The Tommies handed out sweets and cigarettes to people who had not seen such luxuries for years.

Jerseymen soldiers, glad to be home!

The supreme moment of Liberation. The Union Flag is pictured being raised from the balcony of the Pomme d'Or Hotel. Jersey was free once more.

Jersey children see their first Jeep as it drives along Victoria Avenue.

This young lad was discovered in Jersey at Liberation. He was a Russian orphan who had been taken prisoner and been made the mascot of a German unit.

Most of the German soldiers were shipped out of the Island as prisoners of war almost immediately after the Liberation.

These PoWs are being used to clear tree stumps away at the married quarters in Green Street.

Some German prisoners were put to work changing the Island back to its pre-war state. These are digging up the railway lines laid on the Commercial Buildings quayside.

*German
prisoners
painting out
Occupation signs
on house fronts.*

*The legacy left by five years
of Occupation were not easy
to clear. Tank traps on La
Haule slip.*

Huge guns, which the Germans set up to fire on shipping, were unceremoniously dumped over the headland at Grosnez.

The rare sight of a complete German gun in its emplacement before removal.

Light guns were taken out of the Island by barge.

The Germans had burrowed into the Island like moles, creating miles of tunnels. This huge tunnel at St Aubin was put on show to the liberated Jersey people in 1945.

Many tunnels were kept closed for lots of German ordnance was left in them. Some was removed and some sealed underground forever.

A British army three-tonner stands just inside a German tunnel as ammunition is loaded. The officer in charge wisely takes a cigarette break outside.

The late Leslie Sinel, whose Occupation Diaries are the only complete contemporary record of the years of Occupation.

In June 1946 the bodies of 16 American servicemen who had been washed ashore in Jersey and Guernsey were collected by the American army and shipped back to their homeland with full ceremony from British troops and Islanders.

People

These good ladies were collecting for the French Red Cross on 'France's Day' during World War One.

A happy party of Beeches Old Boys and their girls enjoy a fancy dress ball at West Park Pavilion in 1937.

Boys will be girls when it comes to a fancy dress 'beauty' parade at the Bathing Pool in the Thirties.

The pupils of St Brelade's School in 1871 may have been told to 'watch the birdie' but no one remembered 'cheese'.

In 1963 both photography and school discipline had changed – as can be seen by the attentive and relaxed children of Halkett Place Junior School at their prize-giving.

The opening game of bowls at the Sun works Recreation Ground, First Tower, in the 1937 season.

Stalwarts have been taking a Christmas Day dip at the Bathing Pool for many decades. This is the 1955 crowd posing before taking the chilly plunge.

Jersey schoolchildren enact the death of Major Peirson at the Battle of Jersey in the Royal Square, after the famous painting by Copley.

One of the most popular features of holidays in Jersey before World War Two were the beach games organised by hotels. This happy crowd are showing muscles and beauty in 1936.

Christmas is for children and the poor children of Jersey were not forgotten. Toys were collected for them at the offices of the Evening Post *and then distributed.*

Christmas was a very special time for the tiny tots of the Westaway crèche, as can be seen in this picture from 1937.

Father Christmas did not always come down the chimney. In 1936 you could find him handing out presents in the centre of St Helier.

'Is it real?' wonder these two little ones as they pause to look at a lion in Santa's Treasure Island grotto in a St Helier store in 1936.

'You have the dolls house and I'll have the motor car.' Two little souls gaze at the wonders the Christmas windows of 1935 had to offer.

Little Miss Perredes and her horse were 'Good Companions', according to the caption of this 1937 picture.

You can take a horse to the movies but you can't get him to tip a winner. This cinema stunt at the Opera House in 1952 was to promote a racing film.

Young ladies wear traditional Jersey dress for a gymkhana cavalcade in Springfield stadium after the Occupation.

In the Thirties you didn't come on holiday just to relax. You had to get fit as well – as these exercises taking place at West Park prove.

Holiday PT was not all hard work — there were jolly games to play as well.

Casting votes was a serious business for the Little Sisters of the Poor in the elections of 1957.

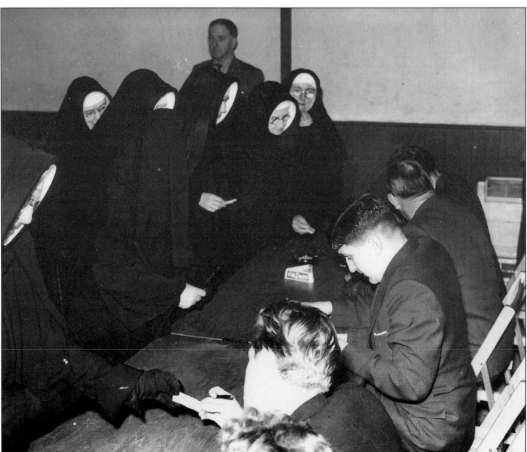

This was an historic rugby match – the last Siam Cup played for between Jersey and Guernsey before the Germans occupied the Island.

Below: Jersey's international junior swimming team, who swam against Wales in 1938.

East meets West in a St Helier store. Persian carpet weavers demonstrate their skills in the window of Le Gallais to the fascination of an elderly gent in 1949.

This remarkable model of the Flying Scotsman was carved from wood by R.C.Lindsay in 1947.

Mr and Mrs Charles L.R.Perrée celebrated their golden wedding in 1948 – and their standard poodle took pride of place.

Left: Young Stephen Deveau, aged five, proudly wears his policeman's helmet and enjoys an iced lolly in the summer of 1972. Right: Beauty parades and competitions were a regular feature at the Bathing Pool during the Thirties.

'John had great big waterproof boots on,
John had a great big waterproof hat,
John had a great big waterproof mackintosh,
And that, said John, is that!'.

When a pram is no good in the snow then how about a carry-cot on runners? An enterprising family cope with icy pavements.

A rare sight in Jersey: snow several feet deep in the harsh winter of 1979.

The strange contrast between the gentle Jersey cow and the harsh lines of German tanks waiting to be scrapped. A bizarre picture taken immediately after the Liberation.

This diminutive 'Austrian' pair were prize-winners in a fancy dress competition at a gymkhana in 1949.

Forty free seats were offered to children who dressed up in cowboy outfits for a performance of the film 'Warlock' at the Odeon Cinema.

The high jump in the schools' sports day at Springfield proves no problem for this young lady in the 1940s.

Tea packing was a light industry which flourished in the Island. These girls are packing Lyons tea in 1956.

A group of women in St Ouen pose in their traditional dress on 'Our Day' in 1916.

This young man is delivering large Christmas trees to the Central Market at the end of the Thirties.

The Marvellous Cinezootrope may have charged only one penny in 1898 but it still seemed short of customers.

Bottles of spirits and dog biscuits could certainly be bought at this emporium proudly decorated with plaques for the visit of King George and Queen Mary in 1921.

A dinghy was the only sensible form of transport in Gorey Village during the severe floods of 1978.

In times past the policemen in Jersey wore a special summer uniform of a white jacket and pith helmet.

Towing away took place in the 1950s as well it seems – although one suspects that this lovely old cab had merely broken down.

One of the great thrills of a day out in Jersey in 1930 was a trip in an open charabanc. This was the Jersey Amateur Fishing Association's day out.

All the fun of the fair for children on the swing-boats in the 1946 fun-fair to celebrate the first anniversary of the Liberation.

Roundabouts and stalls were packed out at the first Liberation Day fair in 1946.

The surfers of St Ouen's Bay show that a surfboard can be used for something other than 'hanging ten' in 1969.

'In the tube' at Grève de Lecq, an example of the wonderful surf to be found on Jersey's beaches.

There was lots of fun to be had in the snow of 1979 if dad gave you a push.

The plane carrying Dot McReady, winner of the Ladies Empire Diving Championship, lands on the West Park beach in 1934.

The beauties line up for the Bathing Pool parade in the late 1940s.

Not to be outdone, the 'beasts' compete as well.

A portable cider-making 'factory' is part of a 1930s agricultural cavalcade at Springfield.

The ladies and gentlemen of Jersey attend a Government House levee for the Sovereign's birthday in 1937.

Waiting for demob in 1945, a returned Jersey soldier indulges in his hobby of painting, much to the amusement of a group of youngsters.

Alphonse Le Gastelois, the 'Hermit of the Ecréhous', who spent years of lonely exile on the tiny reef after being falsely suspected of crimes in Jersey.

The close-knit group of buildings on the Ecréhous reef where Alphonse Le Gastelois spent his self-imposed exile, which began in 1966.

A happy crowd of spectators waits for the 1926 Muratti (the Jersey versus Guernsey soccer derby) to begin.

A glorious display of flowers on the graves of the British and American servicemen whose bodies were washed ashore on Jersey beaches during the German Occupation.

When the undersea telephone cable arrived at Plémont beach in 1938 there were plenty of holidaymakers in their beach clothes willing to heave-ho.

'The King is dead – long live the Queen.' The proclamation of the accession of Queen Elizabeth II is made in the Royal Square on 9 February 1952.

The laying of the commemorative foundation stone of Victoria Pier in July 1887.

2 June 1953 was a great day for children. This street celebrated not only with a party but also a splendid triumphal arch for the coronation of Elizabeth II.

A rare heavy frost turns St Ouen's pond into a cycle track in 1963.

The headstone of the Jersey 'Lily' in St Saviour's churchyard.

Edmund Blampied, painter and etcher, whose works depicting farming life in Jersey are sought after world-wide.

Above: Westward, T.B.Davis' beautiful racing yacht, under full sail. She was scuttled at her owner's request after his death.

Left: T.B.Davis, the great benefactor who donated so much to Jersey, at the wheel of his yacht, Westward. *His gifts include Howard Davis Farm, Howard Davis Park and a lifeboat, all named in memory of his dead son.*

The most appealing bovine in the world. A Jersey calf stands with the farmer beneath a typical Jersey granite farm archway.

A Jersey farming lady proudly shows off one of her fine Jersey cows.

Views

A train waits in the station at Gorey at the beginning of the century, the great pile of Mont Orgueil towering above it.

The Royal Court of Jersey, with a copy of the painting of 'The Death of Major Peirson' by John Singleton Copley.

St Helier shops festooned with decorations for the visit of King George V and Queen Mary in 1921.

The beauty of St Ouen's Manor in the snow of 1947.

The lodge and archway to St Ouen's Manor in the snow of 1947.

Jersey's brand new Airport photographed from the air for the first time in 1937.

Charing Cross in St Helier in the 1930s, long before the main streets were pedestrianised.

The top of Halkett Place, St Helier, in the 1890s, when it was just a narrow lane. The protruding building is being demolished to make way for the wide street it is today.

A bustling King Street, St Helier, in the post-war years when traffic still drove through it.

The children stream out from a Saturday morning kids' cinema at the Odeon, Bath Street, in 1940.

Queen Street at the end of the last century when H.G.Allix, the shop on the left, produced this splendid postcard.

Queen Street, St Helier, between the wars, with a dairy on the left and Boots on the right and traffic going both ways.

Old St Helier contrasts with what were very modern platform soles in 1975.

Mont Orgueil and Gorey under snow in the winter of 1979.

The spectacular fire at Le Gallais Stores in 1954 at its height during the night.

The morning after the fire at Le Gallais rubble fills Bath Street.

The hustle and bustle of King Street, St Helier, in 1955, when pedestrians had to share the street with vehicles.

'Long Live the King and Queen.' The jewellers Maine celebrate the visit of King George V and Queen Mary in 1921.

Rough seas break over the slip at Bouley Bay in March 1952.

The Royal Square, St Helier, filled with loyal Jersey people for the proclamation of the accession of Elizabeth II on 9 February 1952.

The rebuilding of La Rocco Tower, St Ouen's Bay, damaged during the Occupation by German gunnery practice, gets under way.

The German occupying forces used the masonic temple as a liquor store.

The interior of the restored masonic temple in Stopford Road.

The States Building and Royal Court Road filled with politicians' splendid motor cars and seen from an unusual angle in 1960.

Huge crowns hang in King Street, St Helier, to celebrate the Silver Jubilee of King George V in 1935.

The Royal Square, St Helier, before the horse chestnut trees were planted in 1893 and before the the Library and Greffe were built in 1886.

Bathing machines and cricket on West Park beach with Elizabeth Castle in the background around 1900.

Queen Street, St Helier, in January 1963 when there were still traffic-lights at Halkett Place.

The beauty of King Street during a Christmas shopping evening.

A serene country lane in the era when the only traffic was the steady progress of horse-drawn vehicles.

West's Cinema, Bath Street, showing the Jack Palance film The McMasters *in 1969.*

Horse-drawn cabs queue to take the passengers from the mailboat just berthed at the Victoria Pier at the beginning of the century.

A gaff cutter enters St Helier Harbour when sail and steam vessels were to be seen berthed at the piers.

Laser beams fan out over the lights, music and jollity of the Battle of Flowers fun-fair.

A three-masted vessel lies alongside the north end of the Albert Pier with the abattoirs in the background.

Two young women wait for the train to arrive at the Gorey terminus in 1911.

Children play on the beach of the Royal Bay of Grouville with Mont Orgueil in the background around the turn of the century.

Bonne Nuit Bay at the beginning of the century before the hotel was built on the hillside.

A picture of Grève de Lecq taken early in the century, showing the military barracks on the right and the round tower in the centre.

This picture of St Aubin at the turn of the century shows the railway line (now the railway walk) beside the road and the school building on the far left.

The great sweep of St Ouen's Bay seen from L'Etacq with a splendid old Wolseley parked (precariously) on the Le Mont du Valette.

A huge crowd gathered to watch the firework display over Elizabeth Castle for Princess Margaret's visit in June 1959.

Gigoulande Mill, unusual in having two waterwheels, one above the other, was built in 1880 and destroyed by the Germans because escaped Russian prisoners had hidden there.

A typical Jersey farmstead nestling in the valley and photographed in 1932.

Ouaisné and the adjacent common with beach bungalows put up by locals for weekend stays. These were demolished by the Germans because they might have given cover to invading troops.

The Bulwarks, St Aubin, photographed in October 1930.

The steps and promenade at Havre des Pas in the early 1900s.

The Jersey round tower at Archirondel early in the century.

Passengers embark onto the mailboat from the Albert Pier. The vehicle in the foreground pulled by two greys is the Pomme d'Or Hotel courtesy bus.

Those left behind wave to the SS Lydia *as she steams out past Elizabeth Castle.*

L'Etacq, the rugged north-west corner of Jersey.

The Great Western Railway steamship Roebuck *arrives in St Helier Harbour.*

Porters could be hired on Plémont beach to carry ladies with their long skirts through the beach pools. The ladies were held most decorously at arm's length under their armpits.

Two women in traditional dress use a well in Trinity.

Vinchelez Lane, St Ouen, the epitome of the Victorian countryside of Jersey.

Royal Square at the beginning of the century. The horse chestnut trees are already well established.

Victorian ladies are pictured bathing decorously at Grève au Lançon, or Plémont as it is now more usually known.

First Tower in the 1900s, after the Waterworks Company had installed a huge water tower and wind pump .

Route Orange, St Brelade, boasted a fine avenue of pines with a thriving squirrel population until the Great Storm of 1987.

On the night of Thursday 15 and 16 October the Island suffered terrible damage in the Great Storm. The trees of Route Orange were among the thousands brought crashing down.

The railway halt at La Haule with a train standing at the platform.

The beauty of a country lane in the heavy snow of 1979.

HMS Jersey, *the fishery protection vessel, arrives in Jersey in 1977.*

A small boat is left high and dry by Jersey's spectacular tidal range .

Subscribers

Gillian Alce
Robin Allix
John Averty

Rex A Barker
A M Bellows
Ernest F Bertram
Mazel & Ian Bird
Mike Bisson
R E & D M Bisson
C W Blampied
C W Blampied
Peter Blampied
Mr J Blanchard
Paul Boleat

A A Chardine
L R Coenen
Gordon Coombs
Mrs M Corley
N M Crowte
R P Crowte

Elsie & John De Bourcier
Dorothy De La Haye
Beryl M Dimond
David Charles Dowden
Philippa M Doxat-Pratt

Arthur Eden

Mary Gaiger
Alan Graham

Ian Harrison
Patricia Hasler

P I Hingston
Nigel & Maureen Holley
Mrs Mabel Holley
Mary Horsall
Mr J C Huelin

Gerald & Brenda Jacklin
Bernard Jegou
D H Jones

Mr A A Kelly
David Keys

J L Le Breton
Brian Le Breuilly
Sally Le Brocq
Mr Andrew Le Brun
D E Le Cornu
A R Le Couteur
George & Fay Le Couteur
Alan Le Feuvre
Kristina Le Feuvre
C G Le Herissier
R Le Herissier
David J Le Maistre
Jurat M Le Ruez
Stephen Le Rossignol
Kenneth John Le Sueur
Malcolm Lewis
David W Luce
Mrs J Luce
Sybil E Luce

P J McGarry
Miss D C Maddock
Mr B R Maindonald

Mr P Maindonald
David B Mallet
Liam Stewart Mitchell
Veronica Moore
P F Morden MBE

Nancy & Peter Newberry
Betty Nicholson
Edward C Noel
Eric North

N M Parker
Ray Parker
H Parry
J Perree
J Perree
Joan Perrier
Susan & Glyn Perry
Sarah Christina Pexton
Alec Podger
Terry Prior

Mary Quinn

Adrian Renouf
Miss Julie Anne Renouf
Mr & Mrs W B Renouf
Constable J Roche

Philip Sohier
Mrs S Symons

K W Tait
R S Taylor
Mr & Mrs P M Trachy

B M Vardon
David E Vibert

Rupert Wagstaffe
Monica Waller
Frank Walker
Harold Warren

Tony Watton
M J Whitlam
Michael Wilkinson
Alan Wilson
Corinne Wiseman